210 Facts About Billie Eilish

The Unofficial Biography Book Packed with Fun, Curious, and Interesting Content

THIS BOOK BELONGS TO:

_____

Published by VendittoEditore.com

1: Did You Know Billie Eilish Was Born on December 18, 2001, in Los Angeles, California?

That's right! Billie Eilish grew up in the heart of Hollywood, surrounded by creativity and music. Her parents, both artists, encouraged her and her brother, Finneas, to explore their talents. Billie started writing songs when she was just 11 years old—imagine that! Her breakout hit "Ocean Eyes" was recorded in her bedroom and went viral when she was only 14. Now, she's one of the biggest pop stars in the world, inspiring millions of fans like YOU to dream big and be themselves. How cool is that?

2: Did You Know Billie Eilish's Full Name is Billie Eilish Pirate Baird O'Connell?

Yes, you read that right—Pirate is actually part of her name! Her parents let her brother Finneas choose one of her middle names, and he thought "Pirate" was perfect. How fun is that? Billie's unique name reflects her creative and bold personality. Born on December 18, 2001, in Los Angeles, she grew up in a family of artists, which helped her become the musical superstar she is today. So next time you listen to her songs, remember: there's a little bit of pirate spirit behind that incredible voice!

1: Did You Know Billie Eilish Was Born on December 18, 2001, in Los Angeles, California?

That's right! Billie Eilish grew up in the heart of Hollywood, surrounded by creativity and music. Her parents, both artists, encouraged her and her brother, Finneas, to explore their talents. Billie started writing songs when she was just 11 years old—imagine that! Her breakout hit "Ocean Eyes" was recorded in her bedroom and went viral when she was only 14. Now, she's one of the biggest pop stars in the world, inspiring millions of fans like YOU to dream big and be themselves. How cool is that?

2: Did You Know Billie Eilish's Full Name is Billie Eilish Pirate Baird O'Connell?

Yes, you read that right—Pirate is actually part of her name! Her parents let her brother Finneas choose one of her middle names, and he thought "Pirate" was perfect. How fun is that? Billie's unique name reflects her creative and bold personality. Born on December 18, 2001, in Los Angeles, she grew up in a family of artists, which helped her become the musical superstar she is today. So next time you listen to her songs, remember: there's a little bit of pirate spirit behind that incredible voice!

3: Did You Know Billie Eilish Has an Older Brother Named Finneas, Who's Also Her Music Producer?

It's true! Billie's brother, Finneas O'Connell, isn't just her sibling—he's her partner in creating all those amazing songs you love. Finneas writes and produces much of Billie's music, helping her turn her ideas into hits. The duo started working together in their childhood home in Los Angeles, creating songs like "Ocean Eyes" that launched Billie's career. Talk about sibling goals! Together, they've won multiple Grammys, proving that family teamwork can lead to incredible success.

4: Did You Know Finneas is Billie Eilish's Best Friend and Collaborator?

That's right! Billie and her older brother, Finneas, share more than just a family bond—they're a dream team when it comes to music. Finneas isn't just her producer; he's her best friend and biggest supporter. They work together to create those magical songs you love, like "Bad Guy" and "Everything I Wanted." Growing up in Los Angeles, the two spent countless hours writing music in their tiny home studio. Their close connection is what makes their songs so special—they're a true brother-sister power duo!

5: Did You Know Billie Eilish and Finneas's First Song Together Was "Ocean Eyes"?

It's true! When Billie was only 13, Finneas wrote a song called "Ocean Eyes" and asked her to sing it. Little did they know, that song would change their lives forever! Recorded in their bedroom, "Ocean Eyes" went viral online, and Billie's career took off. The dreamy track showcases Billie's unique voice and Finneas's incredible songwriting skills. It's amazing to think that their very first collaboration became such a massive hit. Talk about starting with a splash!

6: Did You Know Billie Eilish Became Famous Thanks to "Ocean Eyes," Released on SoundCloud?

It all started with a little song posted online! Billie and her brother Finneas uploaded "Ocean Eyes" to SoundCloud just for fun, but it quickly went viral. People couldn't get enough of Billie's hauntingly beautiful voice and the emotional lyrics. She was only 14 at the time, and the song turned her into an overnight sensation. From a bedroom recording to millions of streams, "Ocean Eyes" proved that big dreams can start small—and the rest is history!

7: Did You Know Billie Eilish Grew Up in a Family of Artists and Musicians?

It's no wonder Billie is so creative—her whole family is full of talent! Her mom is a songwriter, her dad plays instruments, and her brother Finneas is a musician and producer. Growing up in Los Angeles, Billie was surrounded by music and encouraged to express herself. Her family even homeschooled her so she could focus on her artistic passions. With such a supportive and creative environment, it's no surprise she became one of the most unique voices in music today!

8: Did You Know Billie Eilish's Parents, Maggie and Patrick, Are Also Actors and Musicians?

That's right! Billie's parents, Maggie Baird and Patrick O'Connell, are multi-talented artists. They've both acted in films and TV shows, and they're also passionate about music. Growing up, Billie and her brother Finneas were constantly surrounded by creativity, which inspired them to pursue their own artistic dreams. Maggie and Patrick even homeschooled Billie, giving her the freedom to focus on writing songs and exploring her love for music. Talk about a family full of talent!

9: Did You Know Billie Eilish Was Part of a Choir in Los Angeles as a Kid?

Before becoming a global superstar, Billie honed her voice in a choir! She joined the Los Angeles Children's Chorus when she was just eight years old. Singing in the choir taught her how to control her voice and helped her develop the unique vocal style we all love today. Those early days of harmonizing and learning music were the foundation for her incredible career. Who knew a little girl in a choir would grow up to become a Grammy-winning icon?

10: Did You Know Billie Eilish Started Writing Songs at Just 11 Years Old?

It's true! Billie's songwriting journey began when she was only 11. Her first song was inspired by a class assignment, and from that moment on, she knew music was her passion. With her brother Finneas by her side, she kept writing and experimenting with sounds in their small Los Angeles home. Those early songs were just the beginning of a career that would take the world by storm. Imagine being that young and already creating music that would one day top the charts!

11: Did You Know Billie Eilish Has a Passion for Dance and Took Lessons for Years?

Before taking the music world by storm, Billie spent years expressing herself through dance! She started taking lessons as a kid and loved performing different styles, from hip-hop to contemporary. Dance was a big part of her life and even inspired some of her music, like the emotional movements in her "Ocean Eyes" video. Although she eventually shifted her focus to singing and songwriting, her passion for dance is still a part of her creative process today. What a talented multitasker!

12: Did You Know She Loves Listening to Nature Sounds, Like the Sound of Rain?

Billie finds peace in the sounds of nature, especially the soothing noise of rain. Whether she's unwinding or looking for inspiration, nature's rhythms help her relax and clear her mind. It's no surprise that many of her songs feature atmospheric sounds, as she often draws from the calming influence of the natural world. For her, listening to nature is a way to connect with herself and the world around her.

13: Did You Know Billie Eilish Had to Stop Dancing Because of an Injury?

It's true, and it's one of the challenges Billie faced on her journey. After years of dedicated dance practice, she suffered a hip injury that forced her to stop dancing. It was a tough moment for her, as dance was a huge part of her life. But Billie didn't let it hold her back—she channeled her energy into her music instead. That setback became a turning point, leading her to focus fully on songwriting and performing. Sometimes, life's challenges can open the door to even greater opportunities!

14: Did You Know she is Known for Her Unique Style and Often Wears Oversized Clothes?

Billie's fashion sense is just as iconic as her music! She loves rocking oversized outfits, a choice that's become her signature look. Her bold, baggy clothes allow her to express herself without feeling judged for her body, sending a powerful message about confidence and individuality. From neon tracksuits to quirky patterns, her style is all about breaking the rules and staying true to herself. Billie's wardrobe isn't just cool—it's an inspiration for fans everywhere to embrace their own unique vibe!

15: Did You Know Billie Eilish Wears Oversized Clothes to Avoid Judgments About Her Body?

Billie's bold fashion choice isn't just about style—it's about sending a message. She's shared that she wears oversized clothing to keep people from judging or objectifying her body. By doing this, Billie takes control of how she's perceived and encourages fans to focus on her talent and personality instead of her appearance. It's a powerful statement about self-respect and individuality, and it's one of the reasons so many people admire her. Billie's message? Be yourself and don't let anyone define you!

16: Did You Know Her Favorite Colors Change Often, But She Loves Black and Neon Green?

She's all about keeping things fresh and exciting! While her favorite colors can vary, black and neon green have a special place in her heart. These bold hues aren't just colors—they're part of her identity. From her edgy outfits to her striking green hair phase, she uses these shades to make a statement. Whether she's going dark and mysterious or bright and daring, her color choices always reflect her fearless personality!

17: Did You Know She Dyed Her Hair Neon Green in 2019, and It Became Her Iconic Look?

In 2019, she took a bold step and dyed her hair neon green—and it instantly became a part of her signature style. The striking green roots paired with black ends were impossible to miss and perfectly matched her fearless, rebellious vibe. This look wasn't just trendy; it became a symbol of her individuality and creative spirit. Fans loved it so much that it's now one of her most memorable fashion moments. She truly knows how to turn heads!

18: Did You Know She Later Changed Her Hair to Platinum Blonde?

After rocking her iconic neon green look for years, she surprised everyone by going platinum blonde! The transformation marked a new era in her career and personal style. While still staying true to her individuality, she used the blonde look to express her evolving personality. Fans adored the change, which showcased her versatility and ability to reinvent herself while staying authentic. Whether she's bold and green or classic and blonde, she always keeps us guessing!

19: Did You Know She's an Animal Lover and Has a Dog Named Shark?

She's not just a music superstar—she's a proud pet mom too! Her adorable dog, Shark, holds a special place in her heart. As an animal lover, she often shares her love for pets and even promotes adopting animals in need. Shark, a rescue dog, is a big part of her life, and she's often seen cuddling or playing with him. Her bond with Shark is just another reason fans adore her—she's as kind and caring as she is talented!

20: Did You Know She's Vegan and Promotes a Sustainable Lifestyle?

She's not just making waves in music—she's making a difference for the planet too! A passionate vegan, she chose this lifestyle to protect animals and reduce her environmental impact. She often uses her platform to encourage fans to make eco-friendly choices, whether it's cutting down on waste, supporting sustainable brands, or trying plant-based meals. Her commitment to a greener world shows that being kind to the planet can be just as cool as her music. She's an inspiration in every way!

21: Did You Know She Loves Drawing and Creating Art in Her Free Time?

When she's not making music, she's often found with a sketchbook in hand! Drawing and creating art are some of her favorite ways to relax and express herself. Her artistic talent shines through in her unique style and even in her music videos, where her creative vision comes to life. For her, art isn't just a hobby—it's another way to share her thoughts and emotions. Whether it's through a song or a sketch, she always finds a way to inspire her fans!

22: Did You Know She Has Synesthesia, a Condition That Lets Her "See" Colors and Shapes in Songs?

It's true—her mind is as unique as her music! Synesthesia allows her to experience songs in a vibrant, multi-sensory way. She doesn't just hear the music; she sees it as colors, shapes, and even textures. This incredible ability influences her creative process, helping her bring her songs to life in a way that feels almost magical. It's no wonder her music and visuals are so deeply connected—they're literally intertwined in her mind. How cool is that?

23: Did You Know She's Very Open About Her Tourette Syndrome?

She's not just a talented artist; she's also incredibly brave. She has Tourette syndrome, a neurological condition that causes involuntary movements and sounds, and she's spoken openly about it to raise awareness. By sharing her experiences, she's helped break the stigma around the condition and shown fans that it's okay to embrace what makes you different. Her honesty and strength inspire so many people to be proud of who they are, no matter what challenges they face.

24: Did You Know She Won Her First Grammy in 2020?

At just 18 years old, she made history by sweeping the 2020 Grammy Awards! She won five Grammys that night, including the "Big Four" categories: Album of the Year, Record of the Year, Song of the Year, and Best New Artist. It was a groundbreaking moment that solidified her as one of the most talented and influential artists of her generation. Her heartfelt acceptance speeches and humble attitude made the night even more unforgettable. She truly deserved the spotlight!

25: Did You Know She Became the Youngest Artist to Win All Four Major Grammy Awards in One Night in 2020?

In 2020, she made music history by winning all four major Grammy categories—Album of the Year, Record of the Year, Song of the Year, and Best New Artist—in a single night. At just 18 years old, she became the youngest artist ever to achieve this incredible feat. Her groundbreaking success with her debut album When We All Fall Asleep, Where Do We Go? and the hit song Bad Guy left everyone in awe. That night, she didn't just win awards—she cemented her place as a music legend!

26: Did You Know She Loves Vegan Sushi?

When it comes to her favorite foods, she's all about vegan sushi! She enjoys creative plant-based rolls packed with fresh veggies, avocado, and innovative flavors. As a committed vegan, she finds delicious ways to enjoy her meals while staying true to her lifestyle. Whether it's a classic avocado roll or a unique twist on sushi, she proves that plant-based dining can be just as exciting and tasty. It's no surprise she has great taste—in music and food!

27: Did You Know She's a Fashion Enthusiast and Has Collaborated with Big Brands Like Gucci?

She doesn't just make a statement with her music—her fashion choices are just as bold! As a style icon, she's known for her daring, oversized outfits and unique looks. Her love for fashion has led to collaborations with top brands like Gucci, where she's brought her edgy and creative flair to the runway. From custom pieces to red carpet showstoppers, she uses fashion as a way to express herself and inspire fans to embrace their individuality. She's truly a trendsetter!

28: Did You Know She Has a Huge Sneaker Collection?

She's not just a music icon—she's a sneakerhead too! Billie has an impressive collection of sneakers, featuring some of the coolest and rarest kicks around. From classic Jordans to custom collaborations, her collection reflects her bold and unique style. She's even worked with brands like Nike to design her own sneakers, adding her personal touch to the sneaker world. Whether on stage or off, her footwear game is always on point!

29: Did You Know Her Favorite Sneakers Are Nike and Jordans?

She's all about rocking the classics! Among her massive sneaker collection, Nike and Jordans are her absolute favorites. She loves their iconic designs and how they match her bold, oversized outfits. In fact, she's even collaborated with Nike to create her own unique sneaker designs, putting her personal spin on these legendary brands. Whether it's a pair of Air Jordans or some fresh Air Force 1s, she always steps out in style!

30: Did You Know She's Very Close to Her Family and Friends Despite Her Fame?

Even with her incredible success, she remains grounded and deeply connected to her loved ones. Her family plays a huge role in her life—her brother Finneas is not just her music collaborator but also her best friend, and her parents have always been her biggest supporters. She also treasures her close friendships, making time for the people who mean the most to her. Her loyalty and love for her inner circle remind us that staying true to your roots is what truly matters!

31: Did You Know She's a Huge Fan of The Office and Knows Many Lines by Heart?

She's not just a music genius—she's also a die-hard fan of The Office! She's watched the show so many times that she knows countless quotes and scenes by memory. In fact, her love for the show is so deep that she even sampled dialogue from it in her song My Strange Addiction. Her fangirl moments prove that even global superstars enjoy binge-watching their favorite comfort shows just like the rest of us!

32: Did You Know She Appeared in an Episode of The Simpsons as Herself?

That's right! She made her way to Springfield, guest-starring as herself in an episode of The Simpsons. In the episode, she crosses paths with Lisa Simpson and bonds over their shared love of music. Her animated debut showed off her playful side and her love for iconic pop culture. Appearing on such a legendary show is just another way she's left her mark—not just in music, but in entertainment history too!

33: Did You Know She Loves Watching Animal Documentaries?

She's not just an animal lover—she's fascinated by learning about them too! In her free time, she enjoys watching documentaries that explore the wonders of the animal kingdom. Whether it's about marine life, exotic wildlife, or conservation efforts, she finds inspiration and peace in these films. Her passion for animals and nature shines through in her lifestyle and her advocacy for protecting the planet. It's just one more reason to admire her!

34: Did You Know She's a Huge Justin Bieber Fan and Called Him Her Childhood Idol?

She's always been open about her love for Justin Bieber! Growing up, she was a devoted Belieber, with posters of him on her walls and his music on repeat. Meeting him later in her career was a dream come true—she even collaborated with him on the remix of her hit song Bad Guy. She's shared how much his music inspired her as a kid, proving that even superstars like her have idols they look up to. It's a full-circle moment that shows dreams really do come true!

35: Did You Know She Met Justin Bieber at Coachella 2019, and It Was an Emotional Moment for Her?

Meeting her childhood idol at Coachella 2019 was a dream come true for her! When she saw Justin Bieber for the first time, she couldn't hide her excitement and emotions. The moment was captured on camera, showing her hugging him tightly, almost in disbelief. She's talked about how much his music meant to her growing up, and meeting him was like stepping into a fairytale. The two later became friends and even collaborated, making the experience even more unforgettable for her—and her fans!

36: Did You Know She's Been Open About Her Mental Health and the Importance of Asking for Help?

She's not just inspiring through her music—she's also a powerful advocate for mental health. She's spoken candidly about her own struggles, sharing her journey to remind others that it's okay to not be okay. She emphasizes the importance of reaching out for help and breaking the stigma surrounding mental health. Her honesty and vulnerability have helped countless fans feel less alone, proving that even the brightest stars face challenges—and that seeking support is a sign of strength.

37: Did You Know One of Her Most Famous Songs, Bad Guy, Became a Global Hit?

Her track Bad Guy wasn't just a song—it was a phenomenon! Released in 2019, it topped charts worldwide and became her first number-one hit on the Billboard Hot 100. With its quirky beat, catchy lyrics, and unforgettable vibe, it quickly cemented her as a pop icon. The song's playful yet edgy energy resonated with millions, and it even won Record of the Year at the Grammys. Bad Guy wasn't just music—it was a cultural moment!

38: Did You Know She Wrote Many of Her Songs in Her Bedroom?

Some of her biggest hits were created in the most relatable place—her bedroom! Alongside her brother Finneas, she wrote and recorded much of her music in their small Los Angeles home. The intimate setting allowed them to experiment freely and craft songs that felt deeply personal and authentic. From Ocean Eyes to Bad Guy, those bedroom sessions proved that you don't need a fancy studio to make world-changing music—just talent, creativity, and a sibling who's also your best collaborator!

39: Did You Know She Loves Writing Songs at Night, When the House is Quiet?

She's shared that nighttime is her favorite time to write music. When the world slows down and the house is silent, her creativity comes alive. The peaceful atmosphere helps her focus and connect deeply with her emotions, which is why her songs feel so raw and honest. Those late-night sessions, often in her bedroom, are where she's crafted some of her most memorable tracks. It's just another glimpse into the unique process behind her incredible music!

40: Did You Know Her Musical Style is a Blend of Pop, Electronic, and Alternative?

Her sound is truly one of a kind! She effortlessly mixes elements of pop, electronic beats, and alternative vibes to create music that feels fresh and unique. Her haunting melodies, experimental production, and honest lyrics set her apart in the music world. This genre-blending approach has helped her connect with fans of all kinds, making her songs resonate on a deeper level. She's proof that breaking the rules in music can lead to something extraordinary!

41: Did You Know She's Inspired by Artists Like Lana Del Rey and Tyler, The Creator?

She's often cited Lana Del Rey and Tyler, The Creator as some of her biggest influences. She admires Lana for her dreamy, cinematic style and emotional storytelling, which have shaped her own approach to music. From Tyler, she draws inspiration from his fearless creativity and boundary-pushing production. Both artists have helped her carve out her unique sound—a mix of emotional depth, bold experimentation, and undeniable individuality. It's a blend that's made her a standout artist in her own right!

42: Did You Know She Loves Memes and Often Shares Funny Ones with Her Fans?

She's not just a music icon—she's also a meme queen! With her quirky sense of humor, she loves finding and sharing hilarious memes that make her laugh. Whether it's a funny take on her own music or something completely random, she enjoys connecting with her fans through humor. Her playful side shows that even global superstars appreciate a good laugh and a relatable joke. It's just one more reason fans adore her!

43: Did You Know She Has a Talent for Beatboxing?

She's not just an incredible singer—she can beatbox too! Her rhythmic skills and ability to create cool sounds with her voice add another layer to her musical genius. Whether she's using it to experiment with new ideas or just for fun, her beatboxing talent shows off her creativity and versatility. It's yet another way she proves there's no limit to what she can do!

44: Did You Know She Once Said She Loves Cartoon Lawyers Like Phoenix Wright?

She's got a quirky side, and it shows in her love for animated characters like Phoenix Wright, the iconic lawyer from the Ace Attorney series! She's mentioned how much she enjoys the dramatic courtroom battles and over-the-top antics of these characters. It's just another fun fact that highlights her playful personality and unique interests. Who wouldn't want to yell "Objection!" with as much style as Phoenix Wright?

45: Did You Know She Has a Bright Smile but Also Loves Making Funny Faces?

She's known for her stunning smile, but she's not afraid to let loose and make silly faces too! Whether she's goofing around in interviews or having fun with fans, her playful expressions show off her carefree and down-to-earth personality. She loves to keep things lighthearted, proving that even global superstars don't always take themselves too seriously. Her goofy side is just one more reason fans can't get enough of her!

46: Did You Know She's Passionate About Board Games, Especially Strategy Ones?

When she's not making music, Billie loves diving into the world of board games! She's particularly a fan of strategy games that challenge her to think critically and plan ahead. Whether it's classics like Catan or newer strategy hits, she enjoys the thrill of outsmarting her opponents and having fun with friends and family. For her, board games are a perfect way to relax and connect with loved ones while exercising her creative brain. Who wouldn't want her on their game night team?

47: Did You Know She Loves Collecting Vintage Items?

Billie has a passion for all things vintage! From unique clothing pieces to retro decor, she's drawn to items with history and character. Her love for vintage often inspires her distinctive style, blending modern trends with timeless classics. Whether it's shopping at thrift stores or discovering rare finds, she enjoys the thrill of uncovering treasures from the past. Her collection is a reflection of her creativity and appreciation for things that stand out—just like her!

48: Did You Know She Lent Her Voice to an Animated Project?

Billie has showcased her talents beyond music by stepping into the world of voice acting! She provided her voice for an animated project, bringing her unique personality to life in a completely new way. The experience allowed her to explore a different side of storytelling, showing her versatility as an artist. Fans loved hearing her in this new role, proving that her creativity knows no bounds—whether she's singing or speaking, she always shines!

49: Did You Know She Once Wrote a Song Based on a Dream She Had?

Billie's creativity goes beyond waking life—she's drawn inspiration from her dreams too! One time, she wrote an entire song based on a vivid dream she had. The surreal experience sparked the lyrics and mood for the track, showcasing how deeply she connects with her subconscious. Her ability to turn dreams into music proves that inspiration can come from anywhere—even the most mysterious places, like the world of sleep!

50: Did You Know She Has a Fragrance Line That She Loves to Experiment With?

Billie isn't just about music and fashion—she's also ventured into the world of fragrance! She launched her own line of perfumes, which reflects her personal style and creativity. She loves experimenting with different scents to create something unique and unforgettable. Just like her music, her fragrances are bold and distinct, offering fans a new way to experience her artistic expression. It's another way she's leaving her mark on the world!

51: Did You Know She Loves Listening to Nature Sounds, Like the Sound of Rain?

Billie finds peace in the sounds of nature, especially the soothing noise of rain. Whether she's unwinding or looking for inspiration, nature's rhythms help her relax and clear her mind. It's no surprise that many of her songs feature atmospheric sounds, as she often draws from the calming influence of the natural world. For her, listening to nature is a way to connect with herself and the world around her.

52: Did You Know She Says Her Dreams Are Often Very Strange and Surreal?

Billie has shared that her dreams are often vivid, bizarre, and full of surreal imagery. They're so unusual that they inspire some of her most creative ideas for her music. She's said that her dreams sometimes feel like entire stories, and she loves turning them into songs. Her dream world is a place where anything can happen, and she taps into that imagination to create the unique, captivating music fans adore.

53: Did You Know She Once Said She Was Afraid of the Dark as a Child?

When she was younger, Billie had a fear of the dark, something many can relate to. The nighttime often felt mysterious and a little scary for her. As she grew older, she faced that fear, and it became a source of inspiration for her music. This experience is just one of the many ways she has turned vulnerability into something powerful, showing that even the brightest stars have had their share of childhood fears.

54: Did You Know She Loves Reading Books, Especially Dystopian Novels?

Billie is a huge book lover, and one of her favorite genres is dystopian novels. She's fascinated by the dark, often chaotic worlds these stories create, where characters navigate through broken societies and face extraordinary challenges. These books allow her to dive into thought-provoking concepts and explore the complexities of the human experience. Her love for dystopian themes also influences her music, where she often tackles deep and intense subjects. For Billie, reading isn't just a hobby—it's a way to inspire her creativity and connect with deeper ideas.

55: Did You Know She's a Big Fan of the Hunger Games Book Series?

Billie has shared that she's a huge fan of the Hunger Games series. She loves the intense storytelling and the strong, complex character of Katniss Everdeen, who fights for survival in a dystopian world. The themes of rebellion and survival resonate deeply with her, and she finds inspiration in the challenges the characters face. For Billie, Hunger Games isn't just a captivating read—it's also a source of creative inspiration that aligns with some of the messages in her own music.

56: Did You Know She Has a Collection of Eccentric Sunglasses?

Billie loves experimenting with fashion, and one of her favorite accessories is her collection of eccentric sunglasses. From bold, oversized frames to funky, colorful designs, her sunglasses add a unique touch to her outfits. Whether she's rocking them for a photoshoot or just out and about, her sunglasses reflect her fun, fearless style. They're not just for protecting her eyes— they're an essential part of her signature look!

57: Did You Know One of Her Favorite Drinks is Iced Tea?

Billie has a love for iced tea, one of her go-to beverages when she's looking for something refreshing. Whether she's relaxing at home or on the go, a cold glass of iced tea is her perfect companion. She's shared how much she enjoys its cool, soothing taste, especially during the warmer months. For Billie, iced tea is more than just a drink—it's a simple pleasure that adds to her laid-back, carefree lifestyle.

58: Did You Know She's Participated in Numerous Initiatives to Fight Climate Change?

Billie is deeply committed to environmental causes and has actively participated in several initiatives to combat climate change. She uses her platform to raise awareness about the urgent need to protect the planet, encouraging her fans to adopt sustainable practices. From supporting eco-friendly brands to organizing charity events, she works tirelessly to make a difference. For Billie, taking action against climate change is a way to ensure a better future for generations to come.

59: Did You Know She's Very Close to Her Fans and Calls Them "Avocado Lovers" as a Joke?

Billie has a special bond with her fans, often showing them love and appreciation. As a playful nickname, she calls them "avocado lovers," a fun term that reflects her quirky sense of humor. This lighthearted name shows how much she values her fanbase, creating a sense of community where everyone can share in her journey. It's just one of the many ways she connects with her supporters, making them feel like part of her world.

60: Did You Know She Has a Hidden Tattoo That She Doesn't Show Often?

Billie has a secret tattoo that she keeps mostly hidden. She's mentioned it in interviews, but rarely shows it off. The tattoo reflects her personal style and individuality, much like the rest of her artistic choices. Billie's love for tattoos is well-known, and while this one stays out of the spotlight, it's a part of her that she keeps for herself. It's just another little mystery that adds to her intriguing, multi-faceted persona.

61: Did You Know She Says She Loves the Rain Because It Relaxes Her and Inspires Her to Write?

Billie has shared that she finds the sound of rain incredibly calming. The gentle noise helps her clear her mind and get into a creative headspace. She often turns to the rain when she needs inspiration, as it creates the perfect atmosphere for writing. For Billie, rain isn't just weather—it's a source of peace and creativity. This love for the rain is reflected in her music, where she often captures the soothing, introspective mood it brings.

62: Did You Know She's Really Good at Pranking Her Friends and Family?

Billie is known for her playful side, especially when it comes to pulling pranks on her friends and family. She loves to surprise them with funny and harmless tricks, keeping everyone on their toes. Her sense of humor is one of the things that makes her so relatable and down-to-earth. Whether it's a silly surprise or a well-planned joke, Billie's pranks always show her fun-loving personality and her close bond with the people she cares about.

63: Did You Know She Loves Puns and Wordplay?

Billie has a natural talent for humor, and she's especially fond of puns and wordplay. She loves to experiment with language and create playful twists on words, often making her fans laugh with her clever jokes. Her quick wit is part of what makes her so charismatic, and she's always ready with a fun pun or a silly phrase. Whether it's in interviews or on social media, Billie's love for wordplay adds another layer to her creative personality and keeps things lighthearted.

64: Did You Know She Once Said She Doesn't Like Balloons Because She Finds Them Strange?

Billie has shared that she's not a fan of balloons, finding them a bit odd. Despite their popularity at parties and celebrations, she feels uncomfortable around them. It's one of those quirky, personal preferences that make her even more relatable to her fans. For Billie, balloons just don't hold the same appeal, and she's not afraid to speak up about it, showing her true self in the most down-to-earth way.

65: Did You Know She Loves Decorating Her Personal Space with Fairy Lights and Plants?

Billie has a special fondness for decorating her space with cozy, relaxing touches like fairy lights and plants. The soft glow of the lights creates a calming atmosphere, while the greenery adds a touch of nature to her home. This combination reflects her laid-back style and her love for creating a peaceful environment. For Billie, these small touches are a way to make her space feel more personal and connected to the things she loves. It's the perfect blend of comfort and creativity!

66: Did You Know One of Her Favorite Foods Is Peanut Butter and Jelly?

Billie loves the classic combination of peanut butter and jelly, often enjoying it as a quick snack or comfort food. The rich, creamy peanut butter paired with sweet jelly is a simple treat that brings her comfort and joy. It's one of those nostalgic meals that reminds her of childhood, and it's a go-to snack for when she's craving something familiar. For Billie, there's nothing like the satisfying taste of peanut butter and jelly to brighten her day!

67: Did You Know She Has a Weakness for Scented Candles, Especially Vanilla?

Billie has a soft spot for scented candles, and vanilla is one of her favorites. The sweet, comforting scent fills her space and adds a cozy, relaxing vibe to her home. She enjoys the calming effect of candles, using them to create a peaceful atmosphere when she's unwinding or getting creative. For Billie, lighting a vanilla-scented candle is the perfect way to set the mood and relax after a long day. It's one of those little things that make her feel at ease.

68: Did You Know Billie Has Been Named "Artist of the Year" by Many Major Magazines?

Billie's incredible talent has earned her numerous "Artist of the Year" titles from major magazines and platforms. Her music, style, and impact on pop culture have made her one of the most influential artists of her generation. With chart-topping albums and unforgettable performances, she's been recognized by outlets like Apple Music, Rolling Stone, and many others. These accolades highlight how she's reshaped the music industry, making her one of the defining voices of the 2020s. Her recognition is a testament to her hard work and unique artistry.

69: Did You Know She Sang the Soundtrack for the James Bond Film No Time to Die?

Billie made history by performing the hauntingly beautiful theme song for the 2021 James Bond film No Time to Die. At just 18 years old, she became the youngest artist ever to write and record a James Bond theme. The song's eerie, emotional tone perfectly matched the film's intense atmosphere and earned critical acclaim. Billie's contribution to the iconic franchise marked a major milestone in her career, further solidifying her place in music history.

70: Did You Know She Loves Doing Puzzles, Especially Those with Lots of Pieces?

Billie has a passion for puzzles, and the more pieces, the better! She finds them a relaxing way to unwind and challenge her mind. The process of slowly piecing everything together helps her clear her head and focus. Whether it's a giant 1,000-piece puzzle or even bigger, she enjoys the sense of accomplishment that comes with finishing a complex design. It's one of the many ways she likes to relax and disconnect, showing her love for simple, meditative activities.

71: Did You Know She Wanted to Be an Art Teacher When She Was Little?

When Billie was younger, she dreamed of becoming an art teacher. She was passionate about creativity and loved expressing herself through drawing and other artistic forms. Her love for art has stayed with her throughout her life, even influencing her music and visual style. Although she eventually pursued a career in music, her childhood dream of teaching art shows how deeply creativity runs in her veins. It's clear that art has always been an important part of who she is!

72: Did You Know She Loves Watching Cute Animal Videos on YouTube?

Billie is a big fan of watching adorable animal videos on YouTube! She enjoys the joy and relaxation that comes from seeing cute animals do funny or heartwarming things. Whether it's kittens playing or puppies learning new tricks, these videos help her unwind and bring a smile to her face. For Billie, there's something magical about the simple happiness that animals bring, and she often shares her love for them with her fans. It's just another way she connects with the lighter side of life!

73: Did You Know She Said Her Favorite Superpower Would Be Flying?

Billie has mentioned that if she could have any superpower, it would be the ability to fly. She's always had an adventurous spirit, and the idea of soaring through the sky captures her imagination. Flying would allow her to explore the world from a new perspective and experience total freedom. For Billie, this superpower represents the feeling of escape and the limitless possibilities that come with it. It's just another glimpse into her free-spirited personality!

74: Did You Know She Loves Writing Letters to Her Friends and Keeping Them?

Billie has a special fondness for writing letters to her friends. She finds it a personal and meaningful way to connect with the people she cares about. These handwritten letters are something she cherishes, and she keeps them as mementos of her relationships. For Billie, it's not just about sending a message—it's about preserving a moment and the feelings behind it. In a world of digital communication, she loves the authenticity and emotional touch that comes with letter writing.

75: Did You Know Her First Concert Was When She Was Just 16?

Billie's journey to stardom began early—she performed her first concert at the age of 16. Despite her young age, she captivated the audience with her unique style and talent. That performance marked the beginning of her rise to fame, and it was the start of her incredible career in music. Performing live was a huge milestone for her, and it helped her build the strong connection she now shares with fans around the world.

76: Did You Know She Has a Pair of Socks for Every Occasion, From the Most Outrageous to the Simplest?

Billie has an impressive sock collection that covers all kinds of styles. Whether she's going for a bold, quirky look or just something comfortable and casual, she always has the perfect pair to match her mood or outfit. From socks with fun patterns and bright colors to simpler, more classic designs, her collection shows off her playful and eclectic sense of style. For Billie, socks are just another way to express herself and add a little fun to her everyday look!

77: Did You Know She Loves Tim Burton's Movies?

Billie is a huge fan of Tim Burton's films, known for their dark, quirky, and imaginative style. She's drawn to the unique worlds Burton creates, filled with eccentric characters and strange, fantastical settings. Movies like Beetlejuice, Edward Scissorhands, and The Nightmare Before Christmas resonate with her creative vision, influencing her own artistic work. Billie loves the way Burton's films embrace the strange and beautiful, which mirrors her own approach to music and style.

78: Did You Know One of Her Favorite Movies Is The Nightmare Before Christmas?

Billie is a big fan of The Nightmare Before Christmas, a film known for its unique stop-motion animation and Tim Burton's signature dark yet whimsical style. She loves the movie's creative storytelling and the charming, eerie atmosphere it creates. The blend of Halloween and Christmas themes, along with memorable characters like Jack Skellington, resonates with her, and she often mentions it as one of her favorites. It's a perfect fit for Billie's love of the fantastical and the unconventional!

79: Did You Know She's Obsessed with Vegan Ice Cream?

Billie has a serious love for vegan ice cream! She's always on the lookout for new flavors and brands, enjoying the delicious, plant-based treats without compromising on taste. Whether it's a rich chocolate or a fruity sorbet, vegan ice cream is one of her go-to snacks. Her obsession with it reflects her commitment to a vegan lifestyle, while still indulging in sweet, refreshing desserts. For Billie, vegan ice cream is the perfect way to satisfy her cravings in a way that aligns with her values!

80: Did You Know She Has an Enormous Hoodie Collection?

Billie is known for her comfy and cool style, and one of her favorite wardrobe staples is hoodies. She has an enormous collection of them, from oversized designs to unique, custom pieces. Whether she's relaxing at home or out in public, hoodies are her go-to for comfort and style. Her love for hoodies reflects her laid-back personality and preference for cozy, yet fashionable outfits. They've become a key part of her signature look!

81: Did You Know She Loves Personalizing Her Clothes with Patches and Pins?

Billie enjoys adding her personal touch to her wardrobe by decorating her clothes with patches and pins. Whether it's a jacket, a hoodie, or a bag, she customizes her pieces to reflect her unique style and personality. This creative process allows her to express herself in a fun and artistic way. For Billie, these small accessories are a form of self-expression, adding an extra layer of individuality to her already iconic looks.

82: Did You Know She Had a Bed Full of Stuffed Animals When She Was Little?

As a child, Billie loved stuffed animals and had a bed filled with them. They were her comforting companions and a source of joy during her early years. Her collection of plush toys reflected her playful, imaginative side, which she still embraces today in her music and style. The stuffed animals were more than just toys—they were a part of her world, helping her feel safe and loved as she grew up.

83: Did You Know She Has a Passion for Photography and Loves Taking Artistic Photos?

Billie has a deep love for photography, often capturing moments through her unique artistic lens. She enjoys experimenting with different styles, from portraits to abstract shots, and uses photography as another way to express her creativity. Whether it's a candid shot or a carefully planned composition, she brings her own personal touch to each image. Photography allows Billie to explore the world around her from a different perspective, and it's just another form of art she's passionate about.

84: Did You Know She's a Fan of 90s Fashion?

Billie is inspired by 90s fashion and often incorporates elements from that era into her wardrobe. She loves the bold, oversized styles, vibrant colors, and grunge influences that defined the decade. Whether it's baggy jeans, flannel shirts, or chunky sneakers, her style often channels the laid-back yet edgy vibe of 90s fashion. For Billie, the fashion of that time is not just nostalgic—it's a reflection of her unique, non-conformist approach to style.

85: Did You Know She Has a Special Talent for Mimicking Different Accents?

Billie has a remarkable ability to imitate various accents, often surprising people with her spot-on impressions. Whether it's British, Australian, or Southern, she can effortlessly switch between them, showing off her vocal versatility. This talent adds another layer to her playful personality, and she enjoys using it to entertain her friends and fans. Billie's knack for accents reflects her creativity and her ability to have fun with language and expression.

86: Did You Know She Loves Playing Video Games, Especially Adventure Games?

Billie is a big fan of video games, and adventure games are her favorite! She enjoys immersing herself in story-driven games where she can explore new worlds, solve puzzles, and take on exciting challenges. The captivating narratives and the sense of discovery keep her hooked for hours. For Billie, video games are not just a hobby—they're a way to unwind and enjoy a fun escape into imaginative realms. It's just another side of her creative personality!

87: Did You Know She's Really Good at Making Vegan Desserts?

Billie has a talent for baking, especially when it comes to making delicious vegan desserts. She loves experimenting with plant-based ingredients to create sweet treats that are both tasty and cruelty-free. From cookies to cakes, Billie's desserts are always a hit with her friends and family. Her passion for vegan baking reflects her love for both cooking and her commitment to a sustainable, animal-friendly lifestyle. It's just another creative outlet for her!

88: Did You Know She Once Did an Interview with Her Brother Finneas Dressed as Animals?

Billie and her brother Finneas have a playful side, and they once took it to the next level by dressing up as animals for an interview! The two showed off their fun personalities, sporting cute and quirky animal costumes while answering questions. It was a hilarious moment that fans loved, showcasing their close sibling bond and their ability to keep things lighthearted. For Billie, it's all about having fun and being herself, even in the most unexpected moments!

89: Did You Know She Loves Listening to Music with Headphones While Traveling?

Billie enjoys immersing herself in music through headphones, especially when she's on the go. Whether she's on a plane, in a car, or traveling to her next destination, she finds it relaxing and comforting to listen to her favorite songs in private. Headphones allow her to block out the world and get lost in the music, making travel a more enjoyable experience. For Billie, it's a perfect way to unwind and connect with the music that inspires her.

90: Did You Know She Said She Loves Sleeping Under Lots of Soft Blankets?

Billie finds comfort in sleeping under multiple soft blankets. She enjoys the cozy, secure feeling that being wrapped up in warmth provides. The weight of the blankets helps her relax and get a good night's sleep, making her feel snug and at peace. For Billie, this simple pleasure is an essential part of her bedtime routine, offering her both comfort and relaxation after a long day. It's one of those small things that bring her happiness and comfort!

91: Did You Know She Loves Flowers and Often Uses Them to Decorate Her Room?

Billie has a soft spot for flowers and enjoys incorporating them into her space. Whether it's fresh flowers or dried ones, they add a natural, colorful touch to her room. The vibrant blooms reflect her love for nature and creativity, bringing a bit of brightness and warmth to her environment. For Billie, flowers are not just a decorative element—they're a way to make her personal space feel more peaceful and inspiring.

92: Did You Know She's a Fan of Mystery Stories and Riddles?

Billie loves the thrill of mystery stories and the challenge of solving riddles. Whether it's reading a suspenseful novel or figuring out a tricky puzzle, she enjoys using her mind to unravel the unknown. The intrigue and suspense in these stories captivate her, and she often enjoys discussing the twists and turns with friends. For Billie, mystery and riddles offer a fun escape and an intellectual challenge, adding a bit of excitement to her downtime.

93: Did You Know She Once Adopted a Stray Cat and Named It "Muffin"?

Billie has a big heart for animals, and once, she adopted a stray cat she found and named it "Muffin." The little furry companion quickly became a cherished part of her life. Muffin's name reflects Billie's playful and affectionate side, showing how much she cares for animals in need. This sweet gesture is just one example of how Billie loves to offer her love and care to the creatures she connects with.

94: Did You Know She Loves Collecting Old Vinyl Records?

Billie has a passion for collecting vintage vinyl records. She loves hunting for rare albums, especially those with unique artwork or a nostalgic feel. The tactile experience of holding a vinyl record and listening to music in its original form gives her a deeper connection to the music she loves. Her collection is a reflection of her appreciation for the past and for the timeless sound of vinyl. For Billie, collecting records is more than a hobby—it's a way to explore music history and find hidden gems.

95: Did You Know Her Favorite Classical Artist Is Beethoven?

Billie has a deep admiration for classical music, and her favorite composer is Ludwig van Beethoven. She loves the emotional depth and complexity of his compositions, which inspire her own music. Beethoven's ability to convey raw emotion through his symphonies and piano pieces resonates with Billie, reflecting her own passion for expressing powerful feelings through sound. For Billie, Beethoven's timeless music is a reminder of the universal power of art and emotion.

96: Did You Know One of Her Biggest Fears Is Losing Her Voice?

Billie has shared that one of her greatest fears is losing her voice. As a singer, her voice is not only her instrument but also a major part of her identity and expression. The thought of not being able to sing or communicate through music is something she takes seriously. This fear shows just how deeply she values her ability to create and connect with others through her voice, making it one of the most precious aspects of her artistry.

97: Did You Know She Loves Wearing Bold and Statement Jewelry?

Billie has a passion for big, eye-catching jewelry that adds a bold touch to her outfits. From oversized rings to chunky necklaces, she enjoys accessorizing with pieces that make a statement. Her love for large jewelry reflects her fearless style and her desire to stand out. Whether it's gold, silver, or colorful gemstones, Billie uses jewelry as an extension of her creative personality, making her look even more unique and memorable.

98: Did You Know She Tried Playing the Violin, But Prefers the Piano?

Billie once experimented with playing the violin, but she found herself more drawn to the piano. Although she gave the violin a try, she felt more comfortable and inspired by the keys of the piano, which became her instrument of choice. She enjoys experimenting with melodies and creating music on the piano, which has become central to her songwriting process. Her musical journey shows that sometimes, finding the right instrument takes time, and the piano turned out to be her perfect fit!

99: Did You Know She Wrote a Song Inspired by Her Dog When She Was Little?

When Billie was a child, she wrote a song inspired by her beloved dog. The song was a reflection of her love for her furry friend and her deep connection with animals. Her early songwriting showed her natural creativity and emotional depth, even at a young age. This song, which she wrote in her younger years, marks one of the first times she used music to express her feelings, setting the stage for the powerful, heartfelt songs she would go on to create later in life.

100: Did You Know One of Her Hobbies Is Watching Historical Documentaries?

Billie enjoys watching historical documentaries in her free time. She finds it fascinating to learn about different periods in history and the events that shaped the world. From ancient civilizations to more modern histories, these documentaries provide her with a deeper understanding of the past. Her interest in history allows her to connect with the world in a meaningful way and sparks her curiosity about the stories that have influenced society. It's one of the many ways Billie keeps expanding her knowledge and perspective.

101: Did You Know Billie Has Said Writing Songs Is Like Keeping a Journal?

Billie has shared that for her, writing songs is like keeping a diary. It's a deeply personal process where she pours her thoughts, feelings, and experiences into her music. Just like journaling, songwriting allows her to reflect on her emotions and capture moments in time. Through her lyrics, she's able to express what's going on in her life, making her songs an honest, raw form of self-expression. For Billie, music is a way to document her journey and connect with others through shared experiences.

102: Did You Know She's Passionate About Digital Art and Illustration?

Billie has a strong passion for digital art and illustration. She enjoys exploring different creative mediums, and digital art allows her to express herself in a modern, tech-savvy way. Whether she's designing her own visuals or experimenting with new techniques, she loves the freedom and flexibility that digital art offers. This creative outlet reflects her artistic personality, showing that she's not just a musician but also a visual artist with a deep appreciation for art in all forms.

103: Did You Know She Once Helped Paint a Mural for a Charity Project?

Billie has a big heart for giving back, and one time, she contributed to a charity project by helping paint a mural. The project was aimed at raising awareness and supporting a good cause, and Billie's artistic touch added to the vibrant, impactful piece. She's always used her creativity for positive change, and this mural was just one of the ways she's shown her dedication to helping others. It's another example of how Billie combines her passion for art with her desire to make a difference.

104: Did You Know She Was the First Artist Born in the 2000s to Reach the Top of the Billboard 200 Chart?

Billie made history as the first artist born in the 2000s to reach the top of the Billboard 200 chart. Her debut album When We All Fall Asleep, Where Do We Go? quickly climbed to number one, marking a major milestone in her career. This achievement solidified her as a groundbreaking artist, showing that her unique sound and style resonated with listeners worldwide. Billie's success on the Billboard 200 was just the beginning of her rise to fame as a global music icon.

105: Did You Know She Loves Painting Her Nails in Eccentric Ways?

Billie is known for her bold and creative style, and her nails are no exception! She enjoys painting them in eccentric, eye-catching designs, often experimenting with wild colors, patterns, and textures. Whether it's neon hues, intricate art, or unique designs, Billie's nails reflect her fearless approach to fashion. Her eccentric nail art adds a fun and personal touch to her look, showing that she's not afraid to embrace her individuality in every detail of her style.

106: Did You Know One of Her Favorite Songs Is "Bohemian Rhapsody" by Queen?

Billie has shared that one of her all-time favorite songs is Bohemian Rhapsody by Queen. She loves the song's unique structure, powerful vocals, and the way it blends multiple genres into one epic track. The song's emotional depth and complexity have always inspired Billie, influencing her own approach to music. For Billie, Bohemian Rhapsody is a timeless masterpiece that showcases the limitless possibilities of musical expression.

107: Did You Know She's a Big Fan of Harry Styles?

Billie is a huge admirer of Harry Styles! She's praised his music, style, and unique artistic approach. Billie often mentions how much she respects his ability to break boundaries and stay true to himself, both musically and fashionably. Harry's influence can be seen in Billie's own career, as both artists are known for their willingness to experiment and push the limits of creativity. Their mutual admiration shows how influential they both are in the music industry.

108: Did You Know She Says She Loves Christmas Holidays Because They Make Her Happy?

Billie has shared that the Christmas holidays are one of her favorite times of the year because they bring her so much joy. The festive atmosphere, family gatherings, and cozy vibes make her feel warm and happy. For Billie, the holiday season is a time to relax, reflect, and spend quality time with loved ones. It's a break from her busy schedule and a chance to appreciate the simple pleasures that come with the season.

109: Did You Know She's Obsessed with Unicorns and Finds Them Adorable?

Billie has a playful obsession with unicorns, often expressing how cute and magical she finds them. The mythical creatures represent a sense of whimsy and fantasy that she loves, and she embraces their joyful, colorful essence. Her fondness for unicorns reflects her fun, imaginative personality, and they sometimes pop up in her personal style or social media posts. For Billie, unicorns are a symbol of creativity and charm, and she can't get enough of their adorable appeal!

110: Did You Know She Wrote a Thank-You Letter to Her Fans for Their Support?

Billie has always shown deep gratitude to her fans, and she once wrote a heartfelt thank-you letter to them for their unwavering support. In the letter, she expressed how much their love and dedication mean to her, acknowledging that their support has been a huge part of her success. For Billie, her fans aren't just followers—they're a community that inspires and motivates her every day. The letter was a beautiful gesture of appreciation for the people who've helped her along the way.

III: Did You Know She Loves Traveling and Discovering New Places?

Billie has a deep love for traveling and exploring new destinations. Whether it's a city she's never visited before or a remote corner of the world, she enjoys experiencing different cultures and environments. Traveling allows her to unwind and find inspiration for her music. She often shares her adventures with fans, showing her excitement for discovering the beauty of the world. For Billie, each new place offers fresh perspectives and creative energy.

II2: Did You Know She's Said She Dreams of Visiting Japan One Day?

Billie has expressed her desire to visit Japan, a place she's always dreamed of exploring. She's fascinated by the culture, the food, and the vibrant atmosphere of the country. Japan's unique blend of tradition and modernity inspires her, and she looks forward to experiencing it firsthand. For Billie, Japan represents a world full of creativity and inspiration, and it's a destination she hopes to visit when the time is right.

113: Did You Know She's Very Active on Social Media but Takes Breaks to Protect Her Mental Health?

Billie is very active on social media, connecting with her fans and sharing parts of her life. However, she's also open about the importance of taking breaks for her mental well-being. She understands the pressure that comes with constant online presence and makes sure to step back when she needs to recharge. For Billie, prioritizing her health is key, and she encourages her fans to do the same. It's a reminder that even celebrities need time for self-care.

114: Did You Know She Once Said Her Favorite Dessert Is Chocolate Cake?

Billie has shared that one of her all-time favorite desserts is chocolate cake. She loves the rich, indulgent taste and enjoys it as a treat whenever she gets the chance. Chocolate cake has a comforting, nostalgic feel for her, and it's the perfect way to satisfy her sweet tooth. For Billie, this classic dessert is a go-to for celebrations or simply for a moment of happiness. It's a sweet indulgence that never goes out of style!

115: Did You Know She Has a Secret Playlist of Songs That Have Inspired Her?

Billie has a secret playlist filled with songs that have inspired her throughout her life and career. This private collection features tracks from a wide range of genres and artists, each leaving a lasting impact on her music. She's mentioned that these songs help her find new ideas and stay motivated, offering a glimpse into the musical influences that shape her own unique sound. For Billie, music is an endless source of inspiration, and this secret playlist keeps her connected to the art that fuels her creativity.

116: Did You Know She Says the Most Fun Moment on Stage Is When Fans Sing Along with Her?

Billie has shared that one of the most enjoyable moments for her during a performance is when her fans sing along with her. The energy and connection she feels with her audience in those moments are unforgettable. It's a reminder that her music has resonated deeply with so many people, and the shared experience creates a special bond between her and her fans. For Billie, these moments of collective joy are what make performing so meaningful.

117: Did You Know She Once Held a Mini Concert for Her Family at Home?

Billie has shared that she once put on a mini concert for her family at home, giving them a private performance. It was a special moment where she could share her music in an intimate setting, surrounded by loved ones. This personal concert allowed Billie to connect with her family in a different way, showcasing her talent and passion for performing. For Billie, those simple, heartfelt moments with family are just as important as the big stages.

118: Did You Know She Loves Hats of All Kinds, Especially Big, Soft Ones?

Billie has a strong affection for hats, and she's especially fond of big, soft ones. Whether it's oversized beanies, wide-brimmed hats, or floppy styles, she loves how they add personality and flair to her outfits. Hats are a key part of her unique style, helping her express herself in a fun and fashionable way. For Billie, a good hat is the perfect accessory to complete her look, combining comfort and style effortlessly.

119: Did You Know She Says Her Dreams Are Often Very Strange and Surreal?

Billie has shared that her dreams are often vivid, bizarre, and full of surreal imagery. She describes them as unusual and sometimes difficult to explain, but they spark her creativity. These strange dreams often influence her music, as she draws inspiration from the emotions and visuals they evoke. For Billie, dreams are a mysterious and inspiring part of her life, helping her tap into a deeper level of creativity.

120: Did You Know She Loves Taking Long Walks in Parks When She Needs Inspiration?

Billie finds peace and creative inspiration in nature, often going for long walks in parks when she's looking for new ideas. The tranquility of the outdoors helps her clear her mind and connect with her thoughts. Surrounded by trees, fresh air, and open space, Billie uses these moments to recharge and spark her creativity. For her, taking a walk in the park is not just a way to relax—it's an essential part of her creative process.

121: Did You Know She Once Decorated Her Room with Neon Lights to Create a Relaxing Atmosphere?

Billie loves creating a calming space, and one of the ways she does this is by decorating her room with neon lights. The vibrant glow adds a cozy, yet edgy vibe to her space, helping her unwind and feel at peace. Neon lights create the perfect environment for relaxation and creativity, allowing Billie to connect with her thoughts and find inspiration. For her, the right atmosphere is key to feeling comfortable and inspired in her personal space.

122: Did You Know She Once Said Her Biggest Dream Is to Keep Making Her Fans Happy with Her Music?

Billie has shared that her greatest dream is to keep creating music that brings joy to her fans. She's passionate about connecting with her audience and wants to make a positive impact on their lives. The idea that her songs can make people happy and help them feel understood is something she deeply values. For Billie, it's not just about making music—it's about creating an emotional connection with her fans and bringing them comfort through her art. This vision is what inspires her to continue sharing her music with the world.

123: Did You Know She's Passionate About Collecting Old Black and White Photographs?

Billie has a deep love for old black and white photographs, finding beauty in their vintage charm. She enjoys collecting these images, as they capture moments in history with a timeless quality. The contrast and details in black and white photos hold a special place in her heart, as they allow her to connect with the past. For Billie, these photographs are more than just memories—they're pieces of art that reflect different eras and stories, inspiring her creative vision.

124: Did You Know She Loves Writing Poetry and Often Turns It into Songs?

Billie has a passion for writing poetry, and many of her poems eventually evolve into songs. This creative process allows her to express her emotions and thoughts through both words and music, making her work even more personal. Poetry serves as a way for Billie to connect with herself and her experiences, giving her a unique approach to songwriting.

125: Did You Know One of Her Favorite Things Is Watching the Stars at Night?

Billie has said that one of her favorite things to do is look at the stars at night. The peaceful, expansive view of the sky inspires a sense of calm and wonder in her. For Billie, stargazing is a time for reflection and dreaming, helping her to connect with nature and find inspiration for her creative projects.

126: Did You Know She's a Fan of Horror Movies, Even Though She Gets Scared Easily?

Billie loves horror films and enjoys the thrill of being scared, even though she admits that they sometimes spook her. She's drawn to the suspenseful plots and intense emotions that come with the genre. Watching horror movies allows her to explore her darker side and embrace the excitement of fear, even if it's just for a moment.

127: Did You Know Billie Has Been an Ambassador for Several Mental Health Campaigns?

Billie is passionate about mental health and has been a vocal ambassador for various campaigns. She uses her platform to raise awareness about the importance of mental well-being and the need to break the stigma surrounding mental health issues. For Billie, supporting these causes is a way to help others feel understood and encourage self-care.

128: Did You Know She Loves Leather Jackets, Especially Vintage Ones?

Billie is a fan of leather jackets, particularly vintage ones. She loves how they add a cool, rebellious edge to any outfit. Vintage leather jackets, with their worn-in look and timeless appeal, are her favorite, as they carry a sense of history and individuality. For Billie, they're more than just a fashion statement—they reflect her personal style.

129: Did You Know She's Passionate About Skateboarding, Even Though She Says She's Not Very Good?

Billie enjoys skateboarding, though she humbly admits that she's not the best at it. She finds it a fun and liberating way to express herself, especially as a form of physical activity. Despite not being a professional skateboarder, Billie loves the freedom it brings and the challenge of trying new tricks.

130: Did You Know She Once Painted a Picture Inspired by Her Song When the Party's Over?

Billie once created a painting inspired by her hit song When the Party's Over. The artwork reflected the emotions and themes of the song, showcasing her ability to express herself creatively in multiple forms of art. The painting was a visual representation of the deep feelings she poured into the music, adding another layer to the song's meaning.

131: Did You Know She Loves Listening to Relaxing Music While Reading?

Billie enjoys listening to calming music while reading, finding that it enhances her focus and helps her unwind. The gentle sounds create a soothing atmosphere that makes reading even more enjoyable. For Billie, this combination of music and literature allows her to escape into different worlds, further fueling her creativity and relaxation.

132: Did You Know She Once Said She Dreamed of Being a Mermaid When She Was Little?

When Billie was a child, she dreamed of being a mermaid, enchanted by the idea of living under the sea. The thought of swimming with dolphins and exploring the ocean's depths fascinated her. This childhood fantasy reflects her love for imagination and the dreamy, magical elements that often appear in her music and artistic vision.

133: Did You Know She's Great at Making Up Funny Stories to Share with Her Friends?

Billie has a knack for creating funny stories, often making her friends laugh with her inventive and humorous tales. She enjoys weaving fun narratives, whether it's about her day or an entirely made-up adventure. Her sense of humor is an important part of her personality, and she loves sharing laughter with those close to her.

134: Did You Know She Loves the Sound of Crunching Leaves When She Walks on Them?

Billie has mentioned that she loves the sound of crunchy leaves underfoot, especially in the fall. The satisfying crackle is something she finds soothing, and it brings a sense of peace as she walks. The sound of leaves adds to her enjoyment of nature, and it's one of those small, comforting details she appreciates during her daily walks.

135: Did You Know She Loves Creating Themed Playlists for Every Occasion?

Billie enjoys putting together themed playlists for different moments, whether it's a relaxing afternoon, a fun party, or an emotional evening. She takes great care in curating the perfect set of songs that match the mood and vibe of the occasion. Her playlists often reflect her eclectic taste in music, featuring a mix of genres and artists that resonate with her at the time. For Billie, music is a way to express how she's feeling and to connect with her environment. These playlists are just another way she shares her love of music with others.

136: Did You Know She Loves Succulent Plants and Has Many in Her Room?

Billie has a deep appreciation for succulent plants and has many of them in her room. These low-maintenance, beautiful plants bring a touch of nature into her space, adding to the calming atmosphere she enjoys. Succulents, with their unique shapes and vibrant colors, reflect her love for quirky, natural elements. They serve as both decorative items and a symbol of her love for life and growth. For Billie, her succulents are more than just plants—they're a way to personalize her space and stay connected to nature.

137: Did You Know She Was Inspired by Her Dreams to Write Some of Her Songs?

Billie has said that some of her songs were inspired by vivid dreams she had. These surreal, often strange dreams offer a rich source of creativity, with their bizarre imagery and deep emotions. She takes elements from her dreams and transforms them into powerful lyrics and melodies. Her ability to turn these dream-like experiences into relatable music shows her unique creative process. For Billie, dreams are a way to explore emotions and ideas that she can channel into her work.

138: Did You Know She Loves Colorful and Extravagant Birthday Cakes?

Billie has a special love for colorful, extravagant birthday cakes. She enjoys the fun and creativity that goes into making a cake not just a dessert but a work of art. Whether it's bold frosting, unique designs, or unusual flavors, Billie finds joy in cakes that break away from tradition. The over-the-top decorations and vibrant colors appeal to her playful and imaginative side. For Billie, a birthday cake isn't just about eating—it's about celebrating in style and having fun with it.

139: Did You Know She Once Said Her Favorite Superhero Is Spider-Man?

Billie has mentioned that Spider-Man is her favorite superhero. She admires his relatability and the way he balances his superhero duties with his personal life. Spider-Man's ability to face challenges while staying grounded is something Billie finds inspiring. She has said that she connects with his sense of responsibility and his struggles, making him a favorite character in her world of superheroes. Spider-Man's blend of strength and vulnerability is something Billie admires, both as a fan and a person.

140: Did You Know She Has a Weakness for Gummy Candies?

Billie has a serious love for gummy candies and admits that she can't resist them. From gummy bears to gummy worms, these chewy treats are her go-to indulgence. She enjoys their sweet, fruity flavor and fun texture, often having them as a snack when she's craving something sweet. Her love for gummies reflects her playful side and her enjoyment of life's simple pleasures. For Billie, gummy candies are the perfect treat to satisfy her sweet tooth.

141: Did You Know One of Her Favorite Things Is Receiving Letters from Her Fans?

Billie has shared that one of her favorite things is receiving letters from her fans. She loves reading the personal messages and hearing how her music has impacted their lives. The letters are a way for her to connect with her fans on a deeper level and show her appreciation for their support. For Billie, these handwritten notes are a reminder of the powerful bond she shares with her audience. They're more than just words—they're a heartfelt connection between her and the people who admire her.

142: Did You Know She Loves Slow, Peaceful Mornings with a Good Cup of Tea?

Billie enjoys slow, peaceful mornings where she can relax with a cup of tea. These quiet moments allow her to unwind before the hustle and bustle of the day. The calming ritual of drinking tea helps her feel grounded and ready to take on whatever comes next. For Billie, these mornings are a time for self-care and reflection, a peaceful start to her busy days. A good cup of tea provides the perfect sense of comfort and calm she loves.

143: Did You Know Her Favorite Scent Is Jasmine Flowers?

Billie has said that her favorite scent is the fragrance of jasmine flowers. She finds the sweet, floral aroma calming and soothing, often associating it with peaceful, quiet moments. Jasmine's delicate, beautiful scent captures the essence of nature's beauty, and Billie enjoys surrounding herself with it. Whether it's in candles, perfumes, or simply fresh flowers, jasmine brings her a sense of calm and relaxation. For Billie, this scent holds a special place in her heart.

144: Did You Know She's Very Creative and Loves Making Up Stories to Entertain Her Family's Kids?

Billie has a knack for inventing fun, imaginative stories to entertain the children in her family. Whether it's a whimsical tale or an exciting adventure, she loves to get creative and bring these stories to life. Her ability to weave stories that captivate and amuse reflects her imaginative spirit and love for creativity. For Billie, storytelling is a way to connect with her younger family members and share moments of joy and laughter. It's just another example of her playful, artistic personality.

145: Did You Know She's Passionate About Instant Photography?

Billie has a passion for instant photography, often using Polaroid cameras to capture memories in the moment. She loves the nostalgia and immediacy of Polaroids, as well as the unique, retro feel they offer. Instant photography allows her to create tangible memories from her experiences, giving her a way to look back at special moments. For Billie, instant photos are more than just pictures—they're a form of art that helps preserve moments in a creative way.

146: Did You Know She Once Wrote a Song Inspired by the Sound of the Wind?

Billie has shared that she once wrote a song inspired by the calming, soothing sound of the wind. The way the wind flows and changes direction sparked her creativity and helped her channel feelings of freedom and introspection into music. This inspiration shows how attuned Billie is to the natural world, finding beauty and motivation in the simplest of sounds. The song reflects her ability to turn everyday experiences into powerful artistic expressions, capturing the essence of nature in her work.

147: Did You Know She Loves Album Artwork and Often Analyzes It Closely?

Billie has a deep appreciation for album covers, especially those that are artistically designed. She enjoys analyzing the visual storytelling that accompanies music, finding meaning in the imagery and how it connects to the music itself. For Billie, album covers are an essential part of the overall artistic experience, offering another layer of expression to explore. She often looks at the details in the artwork and interprets how they reflect the themes of the music. This attention to detail showcases her keen eye for creativity and design.

148: Did You Know Billie Has a Secret Passion for Karaoke?

Billie has a secret love for karaoke, enjoying it as a fun and relaxed way to sing her favorite songs. Despite her fame as a professional singer, she loves letting loose and having fun with friends and family, belting out tunes in a casual setting. Karaoke allows Billie to connect with others in a laid-back environment and express herself without the pressure of performing on stage. It's one of the many ways she enjoys music in her personal life, outside of her professional career.

149: Did You Know She Likes Playing Hide-and-Seek with Her Friends?

Billie enjoys playing hide-and-seek, a game that brings out her playful side. She finds joy in the simplicity and excitement of hiding and seeking, often playing with friends and family. The thrill of trying to find the best hiding spot or trying to seek out her friends brings her back to her childhood, where she could enjoy carefree moments. For Billie, games like hide-and-seek are a fun way to bond with the people she cares about and let loose for a while.

150: Did You Know She's a Fan of Retro Video Games Like Tetris and Pac-Man?

Billie is a fan of retro video games, particularly classics like Tetris and Pac-Man. She enjoys the simplicity and nostalgia of these old-school games, finding them both fun and challenging. The straightforward yet addictive gameplay appeals to her, as it allows her to unwind and enjoy a bit of competition. Retro video games are a great escape for Billie, giving her a way to relax while connecting with the past. Her love for these games shows that sometimes, the simplest things are the most enjoyable.

151: Did You Know Billie Once Built a Birdhouse in Her Garden?

Billie once took the time to build a birdhouse in her garden, showing her love for nature and wildlife. She found joy in creating a small home for birds, helping them find shelter and food in her outdoor space. This simple act of kindness reflects her nurturing side and her appreciation for animals. Billie has always shown a deep respect for nature, and this birdhouse is just one example of how she expresses that love in her everyday life. It's a small gesture, but one that brings her closer to the world around her.

152: Did You Know She's Really Good at Drawing Caricatures of Famous People?

Billie has a special talent for drawing caricatures of famous people. She enjoys exaggerating their features in a playful and artistic way, creating humorous and unique portraits. Her ability to capture the essence of a person's likeness while having fun with the details shows her creativity and artistic skills. This talent for caricatures is just another way Billie expresses her artistic side and brings her own twist to the world of visual art.

153: Did You Know One of Her Favorite Memories Is Watching the Sunset on the Beach?

Billie has said that one of her most cherished memories is watching the sunset on the beach. The peaceful moment, surrounded by nature, filled her with a sense of calm and beauty. The sunset, with its vibrant colors and peaceful atmosphere, represents a time of reflection for Billie. It's one of those simple yet powerful experiences that she holds close to her heart, a memory that continues to inspire her both personally and creatively.

154: Did You Know She Loves Collecting Colorful Stickers?

Billie loves collecting colorful stickers, often using them to decorate her personal items or to simply enjoy their vibrant designs. She finds joy in the creativity and fun that stickers bring, choosing ones that match her unique personality and style. Collecting stickers allows Billie to express herself in a playful and artistic way, and she enjoys finding new designs to add to her collection. For Billie, stickers are more than just a hobby—they're a form of self-expression and a way to add color to her life.

155: Did You Know One of Her Favorite Traditions Is Decorating the Christmas Tree with Her Family?

Billie's favorite tradition during the holiday season is decorating the Christmas tree with her family. The activity brings them together to share moments of joy and laughter while creating a beautiful centerpiece for the home. For Billie, decorating the tree is more than just a holiday activity—it's a way to bond with loved ones and celebrate the warmth of family. The tradition adds to the magic of the season, making the time spent together even more special.

156: Did You Know She Loves Listening to Rain Sounds While Writing Her Songs?

Billie has mentioned that she enjoys listening to the sound of rain while she writes her songs. The gentle, rhythmic sound of rain helps her focus and creates a peaceful atmosphere that enhances her creativity. For Billie, the rain's soothing sound helps her connect with her emotions and find inspiration for her lyrics. Whether it's a light drizzle or a heavy downpour, the sound of rain brings her a sense of calm and flow during the songwriting process.

157: Did You Know Billie Once Created a Mini-Album of Drawings for Her Brother Finneas?

Billie once created a mini-album of drawings for her brother Finneas, showcasing her love for art and her close relationship with him. The album, filled with illustrations, was a thoughtful and personal gift that reflected her creative side. Billie has always enjoyed expressing herself through different forms of art, and this mini-album was a way for her to share her love and appreciation with her brother. It's a beautiful example of how she channels her creativity into meaningful gestures for those she cares about.

158: Did You Know She's Really Good at Baking, Especially Chocolate Chip Cookies?

Billie is a talented baker, and one of her specialties is making chocolate chip cookies. She enjoys the process of baking, finding it both relaxing and rewarding. The rich, gooey cookies are a favorite treat of hers, and she often bakes them for friends and family. For Billie, baking is a way to unwind, create something delicious, and share it with the people she loves. It's another one of her many creative outlets that brings her joy.

159: Did You Know She Loves Foggy Days Because They Feel Magical?

Billie loves foggy days because they have a magical, mysterious feel. The soft, diffused light and the sense of calm that comes with fog make her feel connected to something otherworldly. For Billie, foggy days are the perfect backdrop for reflection and creativity. The stillness and quietness that come with fog bring a peaceful, almost surreal atmosphere that she finds inspiring and enchanting. It's one of the many simple joys she enjoys.

160: Did You Know She Participated in a Talent Show When She Was a Kid?

When Billie was younger, she participated in a talent show at school, showcasing her early passion for performing. Although she was still a child, she had a natural confidence and love for music that made her stand out. The talent show was one of her first experiences in front of an audience, setting the stage for her future career in music. It was a memorable moment in her journey, and a reminder of how far she's come since those early days.

161: Did You Know Billie Is a Fan of Fairy Tales and Magical Stories?

Billie loves fairy tales and magical stories, drawn to their whimsical and fantastical elements. She enjoys the creativity and escape that these tales offer, allowing her to immerse herself in worlds of imagination. Whether it's classic fairy tales or modern magical stories, Billie appreciates how they stir the imagination and evoke a sense of wonder. These stories also inspire her creativity, influencing the artistic visions she brings to her music and personal style. For Billie, magic is everywhere, and fairy tales are a timeless source of inspiration.

162: Did You Know She Loves Clothes with Colorful and Original Prints?

Billie enjoys wearing clothes with bold, colorful, and unique prints that reflect her individual style. She loves experimenting with fashion and isn't afraid to stand out with eye-catching designs. Her clothing choices often showcase her playful, creative personality, mixing patterns, colors, and textures in unexpected ways. For Billie, fashion is another form of self-expression, and she embraces vibrant prints that highlight her artistic flair. Colorful clothes are just one more way she demonstrates her fearless approach to personal style.

163: Did You Know She Said She Would Love to Write a Book One Day?

Billie has expressed interest in writing a book someday. She loves storytelling and has a natural ability to capture emotions and ideas through words. Writing a book is something she sees as a potential future project, giving her another outlet to express her creativity. Her love for writing, whether it's songs or stories, reflects her passion for connecting with others through words. A book would be an exciting way for Billie to share more of her thoughts and stories with her fans.

164: Did You Know Billie Loves Picnics in Parks with Blankets and Baskets Full of Snacks?

Billie enjoys the simple pleasure of having a picnic in the park, surrounded by nature. She loves spreading out a cozy blanket, packing a basket full of delicious snacks, and spending time outdoors. Picnics offer her a chance to relax, unwind, and connect with friends or family in a peaceful setting. For Billie, these moments of serenity are a perfect way to recharge and enjoy the little things in life. It's one of her favorite ways to make lasting memories with loved ones.

165: Did You Know She Once Wrote a Letter to Herself to Encourage Her in Tough Times?

Billie has shared that she once wrote a letter to herself as a way of offering encouragement during difficult moments. The letter served as a reminder of her strength and resilience, helping her through challenges. Writing this letter allowed Billie to connect with her inner self and stay motivated. It's a personal, meaningful way she copes with tough times, showing that she's not afraid to take the time to support herself emotionally. This gesture highlights her self-awareness and commitment to mental well-being.

166: Did You Know She Loves the Smell of New Books and Bookstores?

Billie has said that she adores the smell of new books and the atmosphere of bookstores. The scent of fresh pages and the cozy feeling of being surrounded by stories bring her comfort. She finds inspiration in bookstores, where she can lose herself in different worlds and explore new ideas. For Billie, books are not just a source of knowledge but also a way to experience new perspectives. The smell of a bookstore reminds her of the endless possibilities found within the pages of a book.

167: Did You Know She Once Said One of Her Secret Passions Is Creative Writing?

Billie has confessed that one of her secret passions is creative writing. She enjoys expressing herself through written words, whether it's through poetry, stories, or even fictional tales. Writing allows Billie to explore her imagination and emotions in a different way than music. Her love for creative writing adds another layer to her artistry, showing that her creativity extends beyond just music and into the written word. It's a personal passion that reflects her deep connection to the art of storytelling.

168: Did You Know She Loves Funny Hats, Like Those in Animal Shapes?

Billie has a soft spot for quirky, funny hats, particularly those shaped like animals. She enjoys wearing these playful accessories as a way to show off her fun, carefree personality. Animal-shaped hats are a favorite of hers because they add a bit of whimsy and humor to any outfit. Billie embraces her love for these silly, creative hats, using them as a fun way to express her unique sense of style. For Billie, fashion is all about having fun and staying true to herself.

169: Did You Know She's a Big Fan of Animated Series, Especially Adventure Time?

Billie is a huge fan of animated series, with Adventure Time being one of her favorites. She enjoys the show's imaginative world, unique characters, and the blend of humor and deeper themes. Adventure Time resonates with Billie due to its creativity and how it explores complex emotions through fantastical adventures. For Billie, animated series like this one provide both entertainment and inspiration, reflecting her love for art that pushes boundaries and offers new perspectives.

170: Did You Know She Says Her Comfort Food Is Hot Soup in the Winter?

Billie has said that her go-to comfort food during the winter months is hot soup. There's something about the warmth and soothing nature of soup that makes it the perfect dish to enjoy when the weather is cold. Whether it's a hearty vegetable soup or a creamy broth, Billie finds comfort in the simplicity and warmth that comes with a bowl of soup. It's a dish that provides not only nourishment but also emotional comfort during chilly days.

171: Did You Know She Has a Collection of Concert Tickets from Other Artists?

Billie has a collection of concert tickets from other artists, a testament to her love for live music. She enjoys attending concerts and experiencing the energy of different performances. Collecting tickets from these events allows her to keep memories of the shows she's seen and the artists who have inspired her. For Billie, these tickets are not just souvenirs—they're reminders of the power of live music and the connection it creates between artists and fans.

172: Did You Know She Loves Super Soft Blankets and Can't Live Without Them?

Billie has a deep love for super soft blankets and says she can't live without them. The comfort and warmth they provide make them essential for her relaxation time. Whether she's lounging at home or cozying up after a long day, a soft blanket is always by her side. For Billie, blankets are a source of comfort and security, helping her unwind and feel at peace. They're a simple, yet important part of her self-care routine.

173: Did You Know She Once Said Her Favorite Animal Is the Horse, Because It's Elegant and Strong?

Billie has said that her favorite animal is the horse, admiring its elegance and strength. Horses represent both grace and power, qualities that Billie finds inspiring. The majestic nature of horses resonates with her, and she has always been fascinated by these animals. Their ability to embody both beauty and strength is something Billie admires, making the horse a symbol of resilience and elegance for her.

174: Did You Know Billie Loves Watching Funny Videos from Her Fans on TikTok?

Billie loves watching funny videos from her fans on TikTok. She enjoys the creativity and humor that fans put into these videos, often sharing them with friends or laughing on her own. For Billie, TikTok is a fun way to connect with her fans and see their unique personalities come through in their content. Watching these funny videos brings joy and reminds her of the positive, lighthearted connections she has with her fanbase. It's a playful way for Billie to engage with the people who support her.

175: Did You Know She Says One of Her Favorite Spots Is a Small Café Near Her House?

Billie has shared that one of her favorite places to visit is a small café near her home. She loves the quiet, cozy atmosphere where she can enjoy a warm drink and take a break from her busy life. This café holds a special place in her heart because it's a spot where she can feel at ease and unwind. For Billie, it's a comforting retreat from the world, a place where she can relax and reflect. It's one of the little pleasures that adds joy to her everyday life.

176: Did You Know Billie Loves Customizing Her Shoes with Unique Designs?

Billie loves making her shoes her own by adding personal, unique designs. Whether it's doodles, graffiti-style art, or bold patterns, she enjoys using her shoes as a canvas for her creativity. Customizing her footwear allows Billie to express her individuality and stand out with a style that's entirely her own. This creative process is just another way she connects to her personal style, turning everyday items into wearable art. For Billie, shoes are more than just something to wear—they're a form of self-expression.

177: Did You Know She Loves Writing Handwritten Letters?

Billie has expressed her love for writing letters by hand. She finds the process of putting pen to paper a personal and meaningful way to communicate, whether it's with family, friends, or fans. Handwritten letters give her a chance to slow down and reflect, offering a more intimate connection than digital messages. For Billie, this practice of writing by hand is a way to share her thoughts and feelings in a heartfelt manner. It's one of the ways she keeps her creativity flowing off-stage.

178: Did You Know She Once Said Her Favorite Color Changed Every Year?

Billie has mentioned that her favorite color changes every year, reflecting her evolving mood and style. This constantly shifting preference shows her love for change and new experiences, as her tastes and creative vision grow. Whether it's a soft pastel or a bold neon, Billie's favorite color often mirrors the season or the vibe she's feeling at the time. For her, color is another way to reflect her personality and mood, making it an important part of her visual world.

179: Did You Know She Loves Sweets with Colorful Icing and Fun Decorations?

Billie has a sweet spot for desserts with colorful icing and fun decorations. She loves the playful and creative designs that make each treat unique. Whether it's cupcakes with vibrant frosting or cookies shaped into quirky designs, Billie enjoys the artistry that goes into these colorful sweets. For her, the fun and whimsical nature of these desserts makes them even more enjoyable. It's not just about the taste—it's about the joy and creativity that come with indulging in these sweet treats.

180: Did You Know She Created a Playlist with Her Favorite Songs for Traveling?

Billie has created a special playlist filled with her favorite songs for travel. Whether she's on a plane, in the car, or simply daydreaming about new destinations, this playlist helps set the mood and make her journeys even more memorable. The songs she chooses are often ones that make her feel relaxed or inspired, turning every trip into a soundtrack for adventure. For Billie, music is the perfect companion to travel, adding a soundtrack to her experiences and connecting her to the places she visits.

181: Did You Know She Likes Painting Her Nails with Fun Designs?

Billie loves painting her nails with fun, creative designs. Whether it's bold patterns, bright colors, or quirky illustrations, she enjoys making her nails a canvas for self-expression. The playful designs reflect her personality, adding an extra touch of creativity to her overall look. For Billie, nail art is just another way to show off her unique style and have fun with her appearance. It's one of the many ways she embraces her individuality and enjoys expressing herself.

182: Did You Know She Loves Ghost Stories, But Only If She Hears Them During the Day?

Billie has a fascination with ghost stories, but she prefers to hear them during the day when the spooky atmosphere is a bit more manageable. She enjoys the thrill of the supernatural but isn't too keen on experiencing it at night. For Billie, ghost stories are a fun and eerie way to let her imagination run wild, but she likes the safety and comfort of daylight while listening to them. It's a playful, spooky interest that adds to her love for the mysterious and the unknown.

183: Did You Know Billie Once Tried Gardening, But It Didn't Go Very Well?

Billie once gave gardening a try but admits it didn't go as planned. While she enjoys the idea of nurturing plants and creating a green space, her first attempt didn't exactly flourish. Despite this, gardening remains a part of her interests, and she appreciates the calming effect that nature can have. While she might not be an expert, her love for plants and nature remains strong, showing that she's always willing to try new things, even if they don't turn out perfect the first time.

184: Did You Know She's a Big Fan of Origami and Loves Folding Paper into Creative Shapes?

Billie is a fan of origami, the Japanese art of folding paper into intricate and creative shapes. She enjoys the process of turning simple sheets of paper into works of art, finding joy in the precision and creativity that origami requires. For Billie, this hobby is a relaxing and rewarding way to spend her time. She loves the challenge of learning new designs and creating something beautiful out of a single piece of paper. Origami allows her to express herself in a quiet, thoughtful way.

185: Did You Know She Loves Japanese Animated Movies, Especially Those from Studio Ghibli?

Billie is a huge fan of Japanese animated movies, particularly those from Studio Ghibli. She admires the magical worlds, deep emotional themes, and stunning animation in films like Spirited Away and My Neighbor Totoro. The creativity and storytelling of Studio Ghibli resonate with her, and she finds inspiration in the rich, imaginative worlds they create. For Billie, these films are more than just entertainment—they're an art form that fuels her own creativity and love for storytelling.

186: Did You Know She Has a Collection of Quirky, Unique Hats?

Billie has a collection of quirky, unique hats that reflect her playful, eclectic style. From oversized beanies to funky, colorful caps, she loves adding these fun accessories to her outfits. Each hat in her collection is a statement piece, showing off her love for fashion and individuality. Billie's hats are just another way she embraces her creative and non-conformist approach to style. Whether for comfort or flair, her hats are an essential part of her signature look.

187: Did You Know Billie Loves Slow Songs That Make You Feel Calm?

Billie has a soft spot for slow songs that evoke a sense of calm and tranquility. She enjoys the emotional depth and soothing melodies of these tracks, finding peace in their gentle pace. For Billie, slow songs offer a way to unwind and connect with her feelings. These songs allow her to express her emotions more intimately, creating a peaceful atmosphere that she finds comforting. Billie's love for slow music shows her appreciation for simplicity and emotional depth in sound.

188: Did You Know Her Favorite Time of Day Is Sunset?

Billie has said that her favorite time of day is sunset. She finds the peaceful transition from day to night a magical and reflective moment. The colors of the sky and the quiet beauty of sunset help her slow down and appreciate the world around her. For Billie, sunset is a time for introspection and relaxation, a moment to unwind and gather her thoughts. It's one of those simple yet powerful experiences that she looks forward to every day.

189: Did You Know She Loves Taking Photos of Her Fans During Concerts?

Billie loves capturing moments with her fans during her concerts by taking photos. She enjoys connecting with her audience in a personal way, freezing the excitement of the show in pictures. For Billie, these photos are a way to remember the energy and love shared between her and her fans. They represent the powerful connection she has with the people who support her music. Through these snapshots, Billie captures not just a moment, but the bond she shares with her fanbase.

190: Did You Know Billie Is Passionate About Handmade Jewelry?

Billie has a deep love for handmade jewelry, appreciating the creativity and uniqueness that comes with each piece. She enjoys wearing accessories that reflect personal craftsmanship, often seeking out designs that are one-of-a-kind. Handmade jewelry allows Billie to express her individuality while supporting artisans who create beautiful, meaningful pieces. For her, jewelry isn't just about style—it's about finding special items that tell a story and make her feel connected to something truly unique.

191: Did You Know She Said One of Her Dreams Is to Have Her Own Fashion Brand?

Billie has shared that one of her dreams is to create her own fashion brand. She's passionate about expressing herself through clothing and style, and she envisions a brand that reflects her bold, unique approach to fashion. With her keen eye for design and her love for individuality, Billie hopes to create a line that inspires others to embrace their own personal style. This dream highlights her ambition and creativity, showing that she wants to make a mark not only in music but in fashion as well.

192: Did You Know She Loves Watching Fireworks on Summer Nights?

Billie enjoys watching fireworks, especially on warm summer nights. She finds the colors and explosions in the sky mesmerizing and loves the excitement that comes with fireworks displays. For Billie, watching fireworks is a way to enjoy the beauty of the moment and feel a sense of wonder. It's a special way she connects with nature and the magic of the summer season, finding joy in the simple pleasures of life.

193: Did You Know Billie Wrote a Song Inspired by Her Love for Nature?

Billie has written songs inspired by her deep love for nature. Her connection with the natural world often influences her music, as she draws inspiration from the beauty, peace, and serenity that nature provides. Whether it's the sound of the wind, the colors of the sky, or the feeling of being surrounded by trees, Billie channels her love for the outdoors into her songwriting. Nature is a source of calm and creativity, and Billie's music reflects that powerful connection.

194: Did You Know She's Really Good at Cooking Simple, Healthy Dishes?

Billie enjoys cooking simple, healthy meals. She takes pride in preparing food that's both nourishing and delicious, often experimenting with fresh ingredients. Her approach to cooking focuses on creating meals that are easy to make, wholesome, and packed with nutrients. For Billie, cooking is a way to care for her body and connect with herself. It's not just about eating—it's about enjoying the process and feeling good about what she's putting into her body.

195: Did You Know One of Her Favorite Hobbies Is Creating Playlists for Her Friends?

Billie loves creating playlists for her friends, carefully curating songs that match their moods or interests. She enjoys the process of picking out the perfect track for different moments, whether it's for a party, a road trip, or a chill evening. Playlists are a way for Billie to share her love for music and connect with her friends through the songs that speak to them. It's a fun, personal way she expresses herself and shows appreciation for the people she cares about.

196: Did You Know She Loves Writing Motivational Messages for Her Fans?

Billie often writes motivational messages for her fans, encouraging them to stay true to themselves and follow their dreams. She understands the importance of mental health and positivity, and she uses her platform to spread messages of self-love and strength. For Billie, her connection with her fans goes beyond music—she wants to inspire them to be the best version of themselves. Her words are a source of comfort and encouragement for many who look up to her.

197: Did You Know Billie Loves Layered Cakes with Lots of Colors?

Billie loves layered cakes, especially those with bright, colorful layers and fun designs. She finds joy in the vibrant, playful look of a multi-layer cake, making it the perfect dessert for any celebration. The different colors and textures reflect her love for creativity and fun. For Billie, cakes are not just delicious treats—they're a way to bring joy to moments and add an extra burst of color to life.

198: Did You Know She Said Her Favorite Childhood Animal Was the Penguin?

As a child, Billie's favorite animal was the penguin, and she's always loved their playful, endearing nature. Penguins' unique waddling walk and their charming personalities captured her heart. The penguin's strength, elegance, and connection to both land and sea inspired Billie in many ways. For her, penguins represent the perfect mix of cute and resilient, qualities she admires and connects with.

199: Did You Know She Loves Dancing Around the House When No One's Watching?

Billie loves dancing around her house when no one is watching, enjoying the freedom of movement and the joy of expressing herself. She doesn't need a stage to perform—just her own space and music. Dancing gives Billie a sense of release, allowing her to feel uninhibited and connected to the rhythm of the music. It's a private and carefree way she lets loose, without any pressure or expectations.

200: Did You Know She's a Big Fan of Romantic Movies, but Only If They Have an Original Twist?

Billie enjoys romantic films, but she's drawn to those that have a unique or original twist. She loves when love stories take an unexpected turn or offer a fresh perspective on romance. For Billie, these kinds of films provide a perfect balance of heartwarming moments and creative storytelling. She's a fan of romance, but she appreciates when the genre breaks away from traditional formulas to offer something new and intriguing.

201: Did You Know She Once Wrote a Song Inspired by an Old Photograph?

Billie once wrote a song inspired by an old photograph she found. The image sparked memories and emotions that she turned into lyrics. For Billie, photos hold a special power to capture moments in time, and this one particular photo inspired her to write a song that reflected the feelings and memories attached to it. It's a beautiful example of how she channels personal experiences into her music, turning snapshots of the past into art.

202: Did You Know She Loves Soft Fabrics Like Velvet and Silk?

Billie is a big fan of soft fabrics like velvet and silk, appreciating the luxurious and smooth textures. She enjoys wearing clothes made from these materials because they make her feel comfortable and elegant. Velvet and silk are not only tactilely pleasing, but they also reflect her style—bold and luxurious, yet simple. These fabrics add a touch of richness and sophistication to her wardrobe, making them perfect for her unique, effortlessly chic look.

203: Did You Know She Loves the Relaxing Sounds of Ocean Waves?

Billie finds the sound of ocean waves incredibly calming and soothing. The rhythmic crashing of the waves against the shore helps her relax and clear her mind. For Billie, the sound of the sea brings a sense of peace and connection to nature, allowing her to unwind and feel grounded. She enjoys listening to these sounds when she needs to escape the noise of everyday life and find tranquility.

204: Did You Know She Said Her Favorite Marine Animal Is the Turtle?

Billie has mentioned that her favorite marine animal is the turtle. She admires their elegance and strength, as well as their slow, steady movement through the ocean. Turtles' resilience and calm nature resonate with Billie, and she finds them fascinating and beautiful. For her, turtles symbolize wisdom, endurance, and the ability to navigate life's challenges with grace.

205: Did You Know She's a Big Fan of Board Games, Like Monopoly?

Billie loves playing board games, and Monopoly is one of her favorites. She enjoys the competitive and strategic nature of the game, as well as the fun of building properties and collecting money. Board games are a way for Billie to spend quality time with friends and family, challenging herself and having fun. For Billie, games like Monopoly are more than just entertainment—they're a way to connect with loved ones and create lasting memories.

206: Did You Know One of Her Favorite Things Is Receiving Handwritten Letters from Her Fans?

Billie loves receiving handwritten letters from her fans. She cherishes these personal notes, as they allow her to connect with her supporters in a meaningful way. Handwritten letters carry a special kind of warmth and sincerity that makes them extra special. For Billie, these letters are a reminder of the deep bond she shares with her fanbase and how much their support means to her.

207: Did You Know Billie Loves Surprises and Often Plans Pranks for Her Friends?

Billie loves surprises and enjoys planning pranks to keep her friends on their toes. Whether it's a playful joke or an unexpected twist, she loves the joy and laughter that come with surprising people. Her love for surprises shows her playful side and her ability to create fun, lighthearted moments. For Billie, surprises and pranks are just another way to show affection and keep things exciting in her relationships.

208: Did You Know She Has a Passion for Adventure Movies, Especially Those with Strong Heroines?

Billie loves adventure films, especially those that feature strong, inspiring heroines. She's drawn to movies where the main character faces challenges, fights for what's right, and shows resilience. These films provide Billie with excitement, empowerment, and inspiration. For Billie, adventure movies with powerful female leads are a way to celebrate strength, courage, and determination in the face of adversity.

209: Did You Know Billie Said That If She Hadn't Become a Singer, She Would Have Liked to Work as a Screenwriter or Director?

Billie has expressed that if she hadn't pursued a career in music, she would have loved to work as a screenwriter or director. She's always had an interest in storytelling and the creative process behind films. The idea of crafting narratives and bringing them to life on screen excites her, showcasing her passion for all forms of artistic expression. Whether it's through music or film, Billie's creativity and love for art shine through in everything she does. For her, the world of storytelling is as captivating as the world of music.

210: Did You Know She Loves Decorating Her Room with Posters of Artists and Images That Inspire Her Every Day?

Billie enjoys decorating her room with posters of artists and images that inspire her daily. She fills her space with visuals that reflect her creativity and the things that motivate her, turning her room into a personal gallery. These posters and images serve as constant reminders of the artists and concepts that influence her work. For Billie, her surroundings are a source of inspiration, and having these visual cues helps fuel her own artistic journey. The room is not just a place to rest—it's a place that sparks her imagination and creativity every day.

"Be brave enough to be yourself, even when it feels hard. Your uniqueness is your power."

"Dream big and don't stop trying, no matter how impossible it seems."

"It's okay to feel different—being different makes you special and unforgettable."

"Let your heart lead you toward what makes you truly happy and fulfilled."

"Mistakes help you grow, so don't fear them—they're part of your journey."

"You're stronger than you realize, and you prove it every time you keep going."

"Shine your brightest, because the world needs your light to make it better."

"Speak your truth with confidence, because your voice matters more than you know."

"Kindness is your greatest strength; it can change the world one small action at a time."

"Follow what you love, and you'll find the life you've always dreamed of."

"Small steps lead to big dreams, so keep moving forward no matter what."

"Don't let fear hold you back—you are braver than you think."

"Your words have the power to inspire, so use them to spread hope and joy."

"Confidence is believing in yourself, even on the tough days."

"You're never too young to make a big difference in the world around you."

"Love your uniqueness—it's the most beautiful part of who you are."

"Your journey is yours alone, so don't compare it to anyone else's."

"Challenges make you stronger, so face them with courage and determination."

"Your creativity is a gift—don't be afraid to share it with the world."

"Be kind and bring light to others; your positivity can make all the difference."

"Your dreams are important, and you have every right to chase them."

"Every day is a chance to grow, shine, and start fresh."

"Keep learning and exploring, because the possibilities are endless."

"Happiness gives you strength—do what makes your heart feel alive."

"You're capable of so much more than you think—keep believing in yourself."

"Success is about trying again and never giving up on what you love."

"Your smile can brighten someone's day, so let it shine often."

"No one can dim your light—stay true to yourself and keep shining."

What are your goals and the milestones you wish to achieve in the future?

What is Billie Eilish's full name?

_____

_____

In what city was Billie Eilish born?

_____

_____

Who is Billie's older brother and frequent collaborator?

_____

_____

What was Billie Eilish's breakout single that went viral in 2015?

_____

_____

What is the title of Billie's debut studio album released in 2019?

_____
_____

How many Grammy Awards did Billie Eilish win in 2020?

_____
_____

What is the name of Billie Eilish's documentary released in 2021?

_____
_____

Which James Bond theme song did Billie Eilish write and perform?

_____
_____

What unique fashion style is Billie Eilish known for?

What condition does Billie Eilish have that she has openly discussed to raise awareness?

What is the name of Billie Eilish's second studio album released in 2021?

Which family member encouraged Billie to start songwriting at a young age?

What is Billie's favorite color, often featured in her earlier music videos?

_____

_____

In what year did Billie Eilish become the youngest artist to win all four major Grammy categories in a single night?

_____

_____

Which famous artist was a major inspiration for Billie Eilish growing up?

_____

_____

What charity causes has Billie Eilish supported, showing her passion for making a difference?

_____

_____

Thank you for purchasing this book!

If you enjoyed it, sign up for our newsletter at VendittoEditore.com, or scan the QR code below to receive free updates, including coloring pages, quizzes, and more fun facts about Billie Eilish!

Made in the USA
Middletown, DE
21 December 2024

67994105R00068